Job Launch

The ultimate student guide to launch into your career by designing a winning application, impressing at interview and landing your dream job

ROMNEY NELSON

Job Launch

Job Launch

This book is dedicated to the amazing role models I have been fortunate enough to have throughout my career. I will be forever grateful for the guidance, support and most importantly, the encouragement they have provided so I could take on new roles and responsibilities and ultimately, do what I love to do.

TABLE OF CONTENTS

INTRODUCTION

The moment that you see your first pay cheque land in your bank account is a feeling of pure joy and amazement! I recall punching the air with excitement as my first pay as a local paper delivery boy of $22.00 was now sitting there in front of me! I couldn't believe it. As an 11-year-old, $22.00 for the delivery of 800 newspapers was awesome. Mind you, that was in the 1980s.

I recall many of my friends getting their first jobs in labour and hospitality positions ranging from furniture delivery, washing cars, collecting and selling 2nd hand golf balls and cleaning windows. These jobs built up our confidence, provided us with a sense of responsibility but importantly, a feeling of financial independence.

Landing your first paid job can sometimes come from childhood ingenuity such as setting up a neighborhood car washing business, selling your garden produce, babysitting or even dog walking for friends and family. Other times, it could be applying for work at a local store, junior umpiring, or creating a product to sell online. There is such a variety of ways that you can begin to get some cash starting to flow into your account and start your financial journal through casual and part-time jobs.

It all sounds easy and straightforward, but there is a problem and it stems from the lack of career education sessions at school to teach the fundamentals of applying for employment. Many students I regularly come into contact with are missing out on jobs because they have poor applications or they perform poorly at the interview. I feel I have an obligation to fill that void and to help out by bringing my many years of business experience to make a significant difference.

There have been too many applications I have disregarded after only 3 seconds due to minor things such as grammatical errors. They ended up being very costly to the failed applicant and over the course of a career, could amount to a significant amount of money, wasted time and potentially missing out on their dream job

In this book, I have collated all of the experience and knowledge I have from over 30 years of being involved in local and international recruitment, national business roles, executive positions and also as a business owner to help you avoid the same mistakes that I see all too often from applicants. As teenagers, you may not have been provided with the skills or knowledge to apply for jobs correctly and therefore give yourselves very little opportunity to even progress to the interview stage. If you can't get to interview, how will you ever give yourself the chance to land a casual, part-time or full-time job?

I am going to show you all the expert tips, the things you should always do and those that you should always avoid. Ways that you can develop a fantastic resume and make yourself stand out from other applicants. I will give you a clear set of instructions on how to develop a winning cover letter to accompany your professional resume and also links to readymade and professional templates that I have created for you to remove the guesswork.

I will also walk you through the unique

communication and body language tips that will make you stand out from the crowd. I want you to land that job, and I will give you everything you need to be successful. It is just a matter of applying the steps in *Job Launch* to allow you to take flight and secure that job.

I want you to use this book as your career guidebook, read it over and over, download the resume templates and refer to this book each time you apply for a job be that your very first job or the position of your dreams. I want you to avoid being discarded into the waste bin or moved to the email deleted items just because you didn't take the time or make an effort to follow these steps. You can be successful in your applications, and you will have every opportunity to move up the career ladder by using *Job Launch* as your go-to book.

So, we have no time to waste. There are jobs out there just waiting for your application because you are now going to be equipped with the knowledge and professional documentation to make you *STAND OUT* from the crowd!

Our Career Challenge

It has been my experience that the challenges we all face in our teens and early '20s are primarily around trying to work out the career we would like to carve out for ourselves.

In our 30's, we are wrestling with conflicting thoughts of what we are currently doing that will provide the income to support our lifestyle over the next ten years. When we hit our mid 30's to early '40s, we have added pressures such as children, school fees, college fees, increasing utility and shopping bills and so on. As we approach our mid 40's and perhaps early '50s, we also start to think about the lifestyle we would like once we decide to ease off from employment in our 60's to enjoy more travel, flexibility or retirement.

It is so difficult to know the kind of career that will keep us moving towards an area of passion, interest, financial profitability and importantly, one that will provide a positive impact for others. In our early teens, we need to seriously begin to think about the subjects we need to choose that will help us build the academic transcript and skills that will move us forward on our journey. It doesn't matter if you intend to complete a trade apprenticeship, attend university, start your own business or take a gap year once graduating, you still need to choose the subjects or courses that you think will be suitable for you to get a positive start for your career.

What We Will Cover?

I have written and designed *Job Launch* with **7 key elements** in mind that I believe will assist you when commencing your career be that in a casual, part-time or full-time capacity.

1. *Finding your career purpose*
2. *Tips for developing a professional and presentable Resume/Curriculum Vitae*
3. *How to develop a persuasive cover letter for job applications*
4. *Submission and application tips*
5. *How to best prepare and perform at interview day*
6. *Best practice for presentation and communication in interviews*
7. *The best templates that you can use for job applications*

Things to Consider

For the majority of students, choosing a career is similar to throwing a dart with your eyes closed, hoping it will hit the bullseye! Choosing your career is usually a combination of several areas. This may include a general interest in a particular field of work, what our friends and family say we should pursue, and what we think could potentially offer a great salary over the short to medium term. The problem being, students rarely stop, reflect and take the time to think broadly across several areas that will provide greater clarity and confidence in their decision making.

I, like many students, didn't know the initial direction of my career. In my primary years, I wanted to be a builder, in my early teens, a physiotherapist, in my mid-teens, a manager of athletes and throughout my late teens, involved in the sports and fitness industry. The end result had me heading off to university to complete a 4-year Bachelor of Physical Education & Health. This was due to a combination of the grades I received in my final year of high school, obtaining a qualification that had broad prospects and in an area that was in my 'strength zone' with previous experience as a sports captain and school leader.

On reflection, the teaching qualification was an excellent foundation as it allowed me to work on my public speaking, organizational skills, time management, leadership, writing, communication and many others. The point being, although teaching in a school wasn't ultimately going to be a lifelong career for me, I was fortunate that I found in my teens to have elected to pursue an area that I was passionate about, would have a positive impact on others, was enjoyable and permitted me to travel internationally and earn an income at the same time.

The challenge for all of us when we are young is exposure and experience in the career we 'think' we would like opposed to jobs that may continue to stimulate us or potentially lead us along another career journey.

As an example, my career involved many twists and turns that ultimately led me to the path I am now on. You will find that the career path you start on, may not necessarily be the one you remain on; in fact, you may detour from that path altogether.

To provide you with a clear example of this, let me list my casual and part-time employment from the age of 11 to the age of 21 years when I was completing my final university studies. You will notice a wide variety of experiences and each one provided me with great skills that I could use as I progressed to my next casual and part time job.

Job 1 - Newspaper delivery boy
Job 2 - Washing windows for neighbors and family
Job 3, 4 and 5 – Waitering and events
Job 6 - Sales Merchandiser for Coca Cola Amatil

Once I graduated with a Bachelor of Education, I then took on full-time employment in the following areas.

- I taught for 8 years in schools across Australia and the United Kingdom. During this time, I progressed to Head of Faculty positions at some of the leading independent schools.

- Following my career as a teacher, I started my Training and Events business in Queensland, Australia.
- I then secured a job with the Australian Football League and moved into a Football Development Position.
- I remained in that role for 12 months before becoming State Manager for a national and international teacher recruitment business.
- Again, I remained in that role for 12 months and then became State Business Development Manager in a sales position. In my nine years with that business, I progressed to a National Role.
- I then changed companies and was appointed to the role of National Partnership Manager and subsequently to an Executive Advisory position.
- Finally, I decided to follow my passion of running my own business called The Life Graduate so I could dedicate my time to develop a broader global impact with the creation of my books and resources.

As you can see, with an employment history spanning more than 30 years, I have experienced a wide variety of positions, all providing invaluable knowledge, great friendships, opportunities and growth in my professional development. All up, I have had more than 20 different jobs, and this illustrates that where you start, will not necessarily be where you end up. I can almost guarantee that!

Introduction to the 4 P's

I'm now going to run through 4 areas that will provide some guidance to assist with your initial career journey. It is essential to consider these because they will provide you with a strong support base to launch into a career that will ultimately begin the forward momentum and move you closer to achieving your dream job.

I would encourage you to take an hour to contemplate what kind of employment will be right for you. It could be the best hour you have invested so carefully consider your initial plans for your career as it may save you years of frustration and potentially lost time moving in the wrong direction.

PLAN

We all need to develop a plan regardless if it's for travel, studying, growing financially or something else. Planning for your career is no different, but very few people do develop a plan. The 4 P's will help you bring together your plan by giving you an understanding of what you would like to achieve over the next 5 or 10 years. Developing your plan will provide the basic structure for you to follow and help you gain clarity and subsequently have better focus for what you need to do.

Developing your plan doubles up as a goal setting exercise too. This is an area that I specialize in; therefore, I will provide you with four fundamentals of goal setting to assist you for your career and planning.

Step 1: **Initial development of your goals**

Firstly, think about what you want to achieve, and why do you want to achieve it? This is the time to dream big and decide what career goals you are going to pursue. What will help you live your dream life? Identify what you are going to try to accomplish and what steps you need to take to get there.

The following are key questions to ask in this initial phase.

Q. What do I want my career to look like in 5 Years?

Q. What industry do I want to be involved in?

Q. Now or in the future, do you want to work for someone else or start your own business?

Q. What is the positive impact that my position or business will have on/for other people.

Q. What are you passionate about? Remember, you will only excel at what you love to do.

Q. Do you have the necessary skills to transfer this passion into a career? What are they or where do you need to upskill yourself?

Q. What problem will it solve for hundreds if not thousands of people?

Q. Will the potential financial return of your career allow you to achieve your personal and financial goals?

Step 2: Write your goals down

Writing down your career goals allows you to commit them to memory and have an easier time visualizing them. Studies have proven that you are over 40% more likely to achieve your goals if they are physically written down!

Be very specific and not overly broad. You should also include a date by which you will achieve your career goal to give you a sense of perspective and urgency that encourages you to take action sooner rather than later.

Step 3: **Develop your career destination map**
To achieve your ideal career goals, you are going to need a map to guide you. First, have a good idea of what your end goal will look like. Reverse engineer the plan by starting at what your end career journey will look like and then work backward from your goal to plot out the path to success. This route will serve as your destination map that will guide you every day until you reach your goal.

Step 4: **Take action every single day**
Every day should help you move closer to your goals. Any day that you fail to complete your daily habits and goals is a day of lost opportunity. Ensuring each day is filled with activity is the best way to finally achieve your goals and be successful. Identify two to three actions to complete each day, and ensure that you complete those actions by the

day's end. You will proceed closer and closer to your goal without even noticing how far you have gotten.

PERSONAL

Are the career decisions you are making yours or have you been influenced by others? Have you been led down a particular path that you are not comfortable with? Ultimately, the decision needs to be yours, and it needs to sit comfortably with you. As mentioned earlier in the book, the career you start with will not necessarily be the one you spend 30 – 40 years in. Your employment needs to be enriching and will not only allow you to grow but will enable you to help many other people and have a positive impact on their lives.

PEOPLE DRIVEN

As Walt Disney once said, "We don't make movies to make money, we make money to make more movies". The question you need to ask yourself is 'Will your career provide positive benefits to the broader community'? Will it help enrich the lives of others? Will your career contribute to making everyone's lives better in some way?

If you think very carefully, the majority of all jobs do

help others in some way be that very small or very impactful. A nurse, for example, with a 10-year career, will have positively impacted many, many patients. A police officer will protect the security of thousands of people. At the same time, a professional basketballer will bring entertainment to the many fans of the sport.

PLEASURABLE

Research suggests that more than 50% of people are unhappy with their jobs. This generally comes down to several factors including the opportunity for career advancement, the working hours required, commuting time, a sense of being undervalued, stress from their job, their pay, feeling locked into their employment due to financial obligations and their relationships with colleagues. I also think it comes down to a lack of awareness and planning early on in their career. If you want to enjoy your job and ultimately your career, it needs to be pleasurable, and you need to know what role will bring you that happiness.

It is important to note that I am yet to meet a person that at some stage has not felt that it's been a 'tough day at the office'. Employment, regardless of the industry or job, will provide a roller-coaster of emotions at certain times. Ideally, you want a job that has significant more 'UP' days than 'down' days and one that will provide you with pleasure. The 'enjoyment factor' of a job needs to be viewed over a long-term perspective rather than a single day. Remember, never base your satisfaction with a job following one bad day or event.

"Within you right now is the power to do things you never dreamed possible. This power becomes available to you just as soon as you can change your beliefs."

- MAXWELL MALTZ (1899 – 1975)

Your IKIGAI

-Career Guidance-

I'm going to introduce you to a concept that I became aware of many years ago that has helped considerably to provide direction and choose the right path for my career. It is a Japanese concept called Ikigai (pronounced "eye-ka-guy"). There is no direct English translation; however, the rough translation is 'reason for being' and embodies happiness for living. Ikigai provides different areas for you to consider with an intersectional point in the middle of the circles called your Ikigai.

Ikigai is not only used to help guide your career but for many other aspects of your life. I do find the exercise of Ikigai does assist students and young adults in developing better clarity on their ideal career. Each intersecting circle provides the following questions to help with your career decisions:

Q. What do you love to do?

Q. What is your passion?

Q. What is your mission?

Q. What are you good at?

Q. What can you get paid for?

Q. What does the world need?

I would encourage you to complete your answers and determine what your Ikigai is?

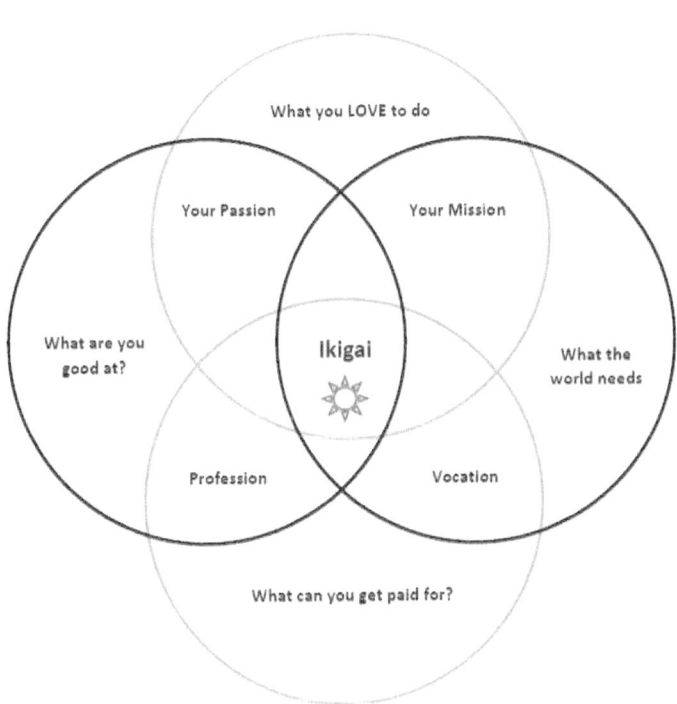

Test and Trial

One final area that I would like to cover is that of testing and trialing different kinds of employment. As I have outlined earlier, my career has been very dynamic, and I have always remained open to various opportunities as they have presented during the past 20+ years.

I have known of people that have completed ten different internships at various businesses in search of a career that they feel would provide the elements outlined in the Ikigai. I am certainly not advocating that you jump randomly from job to job; however, I would encourage you to try to write down a minimum of 20 areas of interest and then narrow the list down to a Top 5 or 10. From this list, investigate if there would be an opportunity to do some work experience or complete an internship. It is a fantastic way to experience the different facets of the job, ask lots of questions from those in that line of work and get an understanding if that would be an area you would pursue. It is far easier to test and trial in your late teens and early 20s than it is in your 30s as greater family and financial responsibilities begin to grow.

Grab a blank sheet of paper and think of all of the jobs that you may like to investigate further. Once you do, list any family, sport or school contacts that could assist with a connection that may be able to assist you. You may need to write some courtesy emails, make some phone calls and arrange the experiences yourself. It may be the best way for you to determine if a particular line of work is going to be right for you without studying at university for 4 years and then finding out the hard way!

The Starting Line

For many students in high school, the prospect of getting employment in either a full-time, part-time or casual capacity will either be daunting, exciting or perhaps a mixture of both. Many students like the idea of developing their own form of financial independence as they transition from their teenage years to their early 20's. Some find it difficult to comprehend life without the convenience of the 'Mum & Dad' bank, and some are forced into various forms of employment through necessity.

Regardless of the reasons, I want to provide you with every opportunity to secure employment and help you on your journey so you can begin to see money steadily start to flow into your bank account and enjoy everything that a career has to offer. To begin with, it is necessary to identify the steps of gaining employment, so I have broken these down into the following five stages.

STAGE 1 - Developing a professional, presentable and appealing resume for submission

STAGE 2 – Writing your cover letter

STAGE 3 – Application submission

STAGE 4 – Job Interview

STAGE 5 – Post interview

The essential tips and information that I will provide will be a combination of my own experiences and feedback from high-level HR Managers and business owners.

STAGE

01

A Professional and Presentable Resume

So many young graduates both in high school and university have such poorly developed resumes they give themselves minimal opportunity to even progress to an interview. This skill can be traced back to limited support or opportunities to learn the craft of resume writing at school or lack of access to professional templates. This is particularly evident if the student wasn't provided with the opportunity to seek assistance from a Careers Guidance Counselor or members of their family.

What is a Resume?

In simple terms, your resume is a written document that effectively provides a condensed summary of information about you. Depending on your location, it can also be referred to as your Curriculum Vitae or C.V for short. This written document is the biography of your education and employment history plus other inclusions such as travel, sports you play, notable publications you have written and any other items that provide a profile of who you are and your background. The document may also have additional inclusions that will highlight key features that complement the position you are applying for

Some people do find it challenging to put together a resume as they feel uncomfortable 'selling' themselves. Well, I'm here to tell you that to land a job or even more importantly a career, you need to become an expert at selling yourself! Nobody is in a better position than you are to talk and write about your strengths, your capacity to exceed the expectations of the employer and become a highly valued employee. Employers will expect you to tell them exactly why you are the best candidate for the job, and you need to develop the confidence to communicate that via your resume.

The flip side for others is they are not sure they have enough content for a resume as they are either still in school with little or no working experience or are unsure how to structure a resume. To help you, I will outline the key components of a resume and those items that would be considered a minimum to include.

1/ Name, Address and Contact Details

In this section, include an email address and contact phone number that you can easily be reached. Ensure that your email address is professional. We will cover that later in the guide.

2/ Education Background

In this section, list your current or previous educational background. This maybe your elementary/primary schooling, high schooling, plus any higher education qualifications you may have.

3/ Qualifications & Awards

List any certificates or qualifications like First aid and sports coaching and list any awards that you may have received throughout school or college. There is no need to list certificates or awards that date back too far as they do become less relevant the older, they are.

4/ Employment History

In this section, note any previous employment be that paid or voluntary. It is recommended you include any work experience that may have been arranged by you or for you while at school. When you list your employment, detail the most recent employment first and then work backwards from there. When detailing any previous employment, list 4 or 5 dot points with some key responsibilities you performed.

5/ Qualities and Attributes

What are your key strengths and what qualities and attributes would you bring to this job? Are you well-organized, committed, have excellent I.T skills or possess great leadership skills? Ensure that what you write down you can back-up as your employer will hold you accountable to what you place in your resume.

6/ References & Referees

A referee is someone that you list on your resume that knows you well and would be happy and available to address any questions that a potential employer may need to know. These questions may include addressing your character, work ethic or experience as a work colleague. When listing your references, you should identify if they are either a character referee or employment referee.

A Character Referee could be a sporting coach or school teacher but shouldn't include any direct relatives like your parents or siblings. Your character referee may not have experience with you in employment. Still, they will know your overall qualities and character as a person.

An Employment Referee will be an individual that has either worked with you as a colleague, manager or as your employer. If you do not have anyone to list as an employment referee should it be your very first application, try to add an additional character referee that holds a senior position of some kind.

By categorizing the two different reference groups, it assists potential employers to contact the right people regarding particular questions and information they may need to know. Choose your referees very wisely. You need to be confident they will speak highly of you and recommend you for the job. Remember, they too will risk their professional reputation when acting as your referee, so don't let them down!

Details of your referee should include their full name, position, title, contact phone number and contact email address. Keep these details current, and it is always polite to notify your referees that they should potentially expect a call if you are applying for jobs or have been shortlisted for a preliminary interview. Usually, referees are contacted following your initial interview and not prior. A courtesy email or call will help your referees to potentially expect a phone call.

Written Reference: You may like to include a written reference to include with your resume. This reference would usually be 250 – 300 words from either a character or employment referee detailing their experiences working with you or outlining your great character. Ensure that this person also signs the document and agrees to be contacted via phone or email if required.

Your Resume Checklist

There are many essential items that you must adhere to when developing your resume. To assist, I have listed an initial 10 that will provide a solid foundation for you.

- Your resume must be free of spelling and grammatical errors.
- Use basic font types like Arial, Cambria or Calibri
- Ensure you avoid flashy headings. Clean, neat and professional is best.
- Dates and listed items must be relevant at the time of submission/application.
- Your resume must be presented on a professional template and saved as a PDF.
- It shouldn't contain more than ten dot points outlining your experience, roles and responsibilities in each of your current or previous positions. The older your previous employment position, the less detail you need

to include.

- You must ensure the formatting of your resume is clean and professional.
- Include Referees. Don't just write 'can be provided upon request' as this may indicate you are trying to hide something.
- Be no more than 3 - 4 pages in length.
- You may like to include a headshot. If you do, make sure the photo is of High-Resolution, you are smiling, it is only you in the frame, and the photo hasn't been cropped to cut someone else out. Worse still, don't use a photo from a party, wedding or a function. The photo should be taken naturally and professionally and with a plain white background and good lighting.

Structure and Layout of your Resume

The layout of your resume is of significant importance. This is the first time that you will make an impression, be that good, bad or indifferent. You can have the most experience, the best qualifications and the greatest referees; however, if your resume looks messy, has poor formatting or looks unprofessional, this will be a direct reflection of you as a person even if this isn't necessarily accurate. From my personal experience, it is usually accurate because if you genuinely care, you will ensure your application is very well presented.

Having reviewed hundreds resumes over the years, there have been many that I have glanced at for less than 1 – 2 seconds. My attitude towards resumes is that if you are not prepared or willing to take the time to develop a professional-looking resume, then this is the effort I should expect if you were to work for me. If it looks sloppy, I expect you will be sloppy and careless too. You need to think of your resume as the paper version of you. Does it shout great organisation, professionalism and care for your work? Does it contain everything that will demonstrate the qualities they should expect from you as a person if they were to employ you?

Headings and Layout

- Keep these consistent throughout the whole document.
- Don't try and be too fancy with the writing styles, colours and graphics. Keep it simple, clean & professional.
- Ensure that the paragraphs are all aligned and

the writing is no smaller than 12 pc.

Format

- I would encourage you to convert your document to PDF format if you are sending electronically. This again will ensure consistency across any device or software used to open up your resume.
- Use simple bullets to highlight essential information. You don't want readers to be distracted from the content.

Remember the 3 tips for resumes
PROFESSIONAL, PRESENTABLE
&
CONVERT TO PFD

*Please refer to Appendix 3 for an example resume template and a link to download your personal copy.

STAGE

02

How to Develop a Cover Letter

A cover letter is generally a 1-page document that will complement your application and could be considered as a synopsis or outline of the key points from your resume. Your cover letter is tailored specifically for the position you are applying for and not a copy & paste from previous applications. Far too many applicants underestimate the importance of this document, and it can be the separation point between the top 10% of applicants to the bottom 90% by just spending time to craft your cover letter for the position.

Most employers will read your cover letter before your resume and if they like what they see, will investigate your application further. If they find your cover letter is too generic and recycled from other applications, you risk being discarded. Further to this, applicants that don't include a cover letter unless specifically requested not to do so, run the risk of not progressing past the initial review process too.

Refer to *Appendix 1* > Cover Letter Template
Refer to *Appendix 2* > Cover Letter Example

Your Cover Letter
Checklist

- If you are serious about a job application, take the time to specifically 'tailor' the cover letter to the position. It may take you an hour to draft, but it may be worth thousands, if not hundreds of thousands of dollars over your career journey if you are successful. From experience and as a senior manager reviewing applications, those that take their time to tailor applications stand out 10x compared to the rest. It demonstrates professionalism and respect for the position, your application and the employer.

- Ensure the letter is free of grammatical errors, and it is well-formatted.

- Avoid exceeding 1 page in length unless you feel that all information is critical to the success of your application.

· Your cover letter is a summary of why you are applying for the position, not an opportunity to give your life story. Your resume is the document that will contain all the critical information. Keep it professional and brief and make sure you make reference to the position title you are applying for and include the employer's name.

Key Tips:

✓ Remember to remove any previous references to any other position you have used this cover letter for. I have personally dismissed applications immediately for the candidate incorrectly leaving the name of a business they have previously applied for in their cover letter.

✓ Read your cover letter out loud or give it to a couple of people to help review it for you. This is a great way to pick up any errors or oversights as the employer may not continue to review your resume if your cover letter is poorly written.

Addressing Selection Criteria for applications

There will be some job applications that require you to address specific *Selection Criteria*. Selection Criteria are questions that will require you to answer in detail information that is specific to the role. It is unlikely that junior positions will require you to address selection criteria; however, it is important to know the following information should you ever be requested to do so.

- If the job advertisement requests you to address the Selection Criteria, then ensure you do. The employer has deliberately requested you address these areas as they are essential for the role. In my experience, those that decide to overlook addressing this information as part of their application are rejected immediately.

- Depending on the question you are asked, it is unlikely you will need to exceed 250 – 300 words per answer. Do not make your application into a 3,000-word essay.

- Use clear formatting and headings on your document so the reader can identify the selection criteria you are addressing.

STAGE

03

Submission of Your Application

To provide you with some helpful hints on your application, I have outlined the key criteria you will need to consider. Most forget that your application will be the first time your employer with receive any correspondence from you unless you have previously applied for a position at that business. Remember, first impressions do count.

Some people like to personally print off hard-copies and walk the streets to hand in their resumes. This will work for smaller businesses, but the majority of all larger businesses have moved to online employment platforms.

My nephew of 19yrs has recently been looking for work, and he mentioned that the online submissions had been the most successful for him. He was encouraged by the larger businesses to submit his expression of interest for employment via the business website jobs portal rather than hand resumes in personally. If you are thinking of applying for a position with a large organisation, first check to see if they have a 'Careers' or 'Jobs' section on their website that you can upload your CV and cover letter directly too as an alternative to posting or handing in resumes in person. The risk with hardcopies is that they may never be passed onto the Human Resources Department or reach the right person unless it is a small business.

TIPS

✓ Be timely with your application. You are best positioned for an interview if you avoid being too close to the cut-off day. Some businesses may begin their shortlisting from the day they list the job and have even finalised interviewing within the first week of applications closing depending on their requirement to fill the position urgently.

✓ If submitting your application online, be mindful of the email address that you use. For example, applying for a job with an email address of camelbreath31@gmail.com may not be viewed as professional nor suitable. Although it may be considered minor, inappropriate email addresses are to be avoided at all costs.

✓ An online application will require a Subject Heading and some brief information included in the body of the email. Your resume and cover letter should do all the talking for your application, so keep this information professional but brief.

Email TIP
An example of a job application to the local Surf Shop.

Subject Heading:
Position Application for Sandy's Surf and Apparel

Dear Sandy,

Please find attached the details regarding my application for the position of Shop Assistant as currently advertised on your website. I have attached the following documents to support my application:

- Cover Letter
- Resume

Should you require any further details then please let me know.

Kind Regards,
Jason Hughes

- ✓ If submitting via post, pay extra for postal tracking to have peace of mind that your application has been delivered successfully.
- ✓ If submitting in person, ensure you dress professionally and make a positive impression with reception staff.
- ✓ Tip: Never underestimate the influence of a receptionist or secretary with your application. They do control the majority of communications across the businesses and serve as the gatekeeper to senior management.
- ✓ If submitting online, keep a copy of the submission receipt number if provided.

STAGE

04

You Have Been Shortlisted for Interview

The prospective employer has been impressed by your initial application, and you have been shortlisted for an interview. This also confirms that your cover letter and resume provided the initial details that your potential employer was looking for and they feel you could be suitable for the position.

You are now given the opportunity to converse in person, via phone or online. Some jobs require a single interview while others may require 2 or 3 stages, including practical scenarios and online courses to determine your suitability. Some businesses require you to undergo a personality test. These tests are used to gain an insight into your work style preferences and are not a comprehensive or complete judgment of you as a person so don't be worried about these.

So, you have been shortlisted for Interview – What to do now?

At this point in the process, you need to be on the front foot and ready to take any action that is required before the interview day. It is often at this stage that many people let themselves down, so I'm here to provide you with some support and guidance. I want you to do all the right things so the moment you walk in for your interview, the interviewers are already impressed!

Here are my Top 5 Tips to impress prior to your interview

1. If you are contacted via email or phone by a prospective employer with a question or a request for further information, ensure you reply as soon as possible. A response later than close of business on the same day will jeopardize your application. It's comical when I see applicants place 'excellent communication skills' or 'timely & efficient' on their C.V if they are not even capable of responding to an employer's request for information in a timely fashion.

2. If you apply for a position, check your phone and emails a couple of times a day just in case you need to respond. If you do need to reply and you use your smartphone, take care with spelling and grammatical errors. You need to be prompt but don't rush it and risk making an error that could

impact your chances. Warning: Don't use emoji' of any kind! ☺

3. Should you receive a phone message regarding your application, take a written note of the details including the name of the person, the request and phone or email information. I recently had a student in one of my sessions that was applying for a position at a large department store. He received a message regarding his application to call to make arrangements for his interview. He didn't take any written notes and accidentally deleted the phone message. When he tried calling the large department store back, they were unable to connect him again with the person that left the message, and his application didn't proceed any further.

4. This is just a general tip but equally as important in these circumstances is regarding your phone message for missed or unanswered calls. I would recommend you create a professional and straightforward voice message. As previously mentioned, first impressions count, and if you are unprofessional on your voicemail, that will

create a negative first impression from the very beginning. Equally as unprofessional, is the automatic phone carrier message when you are asked by a robotic voice to leave a 10-second message that will be sent as an SMS/TXT message.

5. I suggest your message says "hello, you have contacted Jason. I'm sorry I'm unable to take your call right now. Please leave a message including a contact number and I will return your call as soon as possible. Thank you."

6. If you have an unprofessional voice message on your phone right now, then *STOP* reading and change this immediately.

7. Organise 24hrs in advance of your interview any paperwork such as certificates, written references and a copy of your resume that you will take. Arrange them neatly in a file or display folder that is easily accessible during the interview. You want to avoid the last-minute search for qualification certificates on the day of the interview.

STAGE

05

Interview Day

Over many years, I have been involved with many standout interviews but also those that I would prefer to forget. Some feel more confident in interviews than others, and it can simply come down to your experience and approach on the day. I've known of interviews where it's almost like a 'speed dating' scenario, and you have approximately 5 minutes to impress before you're moved on to the next table, or your interview concludes. Others can involve an initial 30 to 60-minute interview and then you may even be asked on the day to complete a further 1-hour unpaid trial in the role to see how you perform. This opportunity is equally as important for you as it will provide the chance for you to see if you would enjoy the position.

The day of any interview will usually produce a few butterflies in the stomach. This is natural and expected. To help ease some of your nerves, make sure that you arrive to your interview location well in advance. This way, you will be on time for the interview and allow you to read over any notes you have, run through some of your responses to potential questions and even go for a short walk.

A message from above!

I would love to share a funny story with you from my personal interview experience when I was shortlisted for my very first teaching position at a prestigious high school. I tried to do all the right things by arriving 30 minutes before the interview, I had read over my notes, and I was relaxed and settled. I still had 20 minutes before my interview, so I thought I would go for a short walk. Little did I know that my 10-minute walk would create such a huge discussion point in my interview!

I got out of my car, went for a short 10-minute stroll, returned to my car, collected the spare copy of my resume and folder containing my university certificates and written references and headed into the foyer of the school administration. I introduced myself to the receptionist, who kindly asked me to take a seat. I noticed that she took a second 'puzzled' glance at me as I turned to take a seat on the leather chesterfield couch.

One of the interview panel members walked out and we shook hands. He kindly pointed in the direction of the principal's office, where the interview was being conducted. I walked in; we said some pleasantries and I introduced myself to all three-panel members.

The school principal who was sitting to my right, lifted his index finger and pointed to my right shoulder 'I'm sorry to tell you Romney, but it looks like a bird has unfortunately made a deposit on your shoulder'! I gave a very nervous smile and looked to my right. To my horror, there was a half green, half white bird poo sitting proudly for the world to see on my suit jacket. All I could do was laugh as I couldn't flick it off and we couldn't continue until it was gone. One of the panel members kindly passed me a tissue and I wiped off what I could and removed my jacket. I had to break the awkward tension so I said: "Well, they do say that a bird pooing on your shoulder is good luck, so I'm looking forward to the interview"! We all started laughing. It was the best ice-breaker possible. And yes, I got the job!

Each interview that you attend will be different depending on if it is a one on one interview or an interview consisting of a panel. The personality types of those interviewing you will also be different; therefore, you need to go with the flow and be very adaptable.

The Top Interview Tips

o ALWAYS be 5 minutes early for your interview. Ten minutes is borderline early as you don't want to be a nuisance and waiting for too long, particularly if interviews are being conducted before yours.

o Check and double-check the location and time of your interview. You get one opportunity at the interview and having the wrong time or location would end things before you even get going.

o If you think it's appropriate, it may also be courteous to email the interviewer the day before to confirm the interview details (time & location) and your attendance.

o Dress appropriately for the interview. It's better

to overdress than under-dress as first impressions count. Don't wear too much jewellery, remove tongue, cheek or nose piercings, cover tattoos as best you can and wear a small amount of cologne or perfume so as not to overpower the interview room.

○ Be well-groomed. Ensure your hair is neat; makeup is suitable and complete a final mirror check.

○ If you decide not to proceed to the interview stage and you have a change of heart, *YOU MUST* contact the employer with plenty of notice. It's incredibly disrespectful to not show up on the day and waste everyone's time. You never know who they might know that could impact future applications.

○ When arriving for the interview, shake hands with all interviewers and say their name. Eg. "Hello Scott, nice to meet you."

○ Remember the names of those interviewing you. If you can, try and repeat their name/s by using them in conversation. If you have a note pad, write them down or get clarification of their name when shaking hands if you feel you have misheard them.

o Come prepared for the interview even if it's just a small folder with a few copies of your resume. If you have gone to the effort of printing off details of the business you are applying for, this will stand out.

o Approach the interview like you're going out for a friendly dinner. You need to be relaxed, friendly and calm. Ultimately, you want those interviewing you to say post-interview "it is like I've known Sally for years. She was so easy to interview".

o Use good posture in the interview. Sit forward on your chair, both hands on the table and share the eye contact across all people that are interviewing you. It's not polite to just maintain eye contact with one person, regardless of their position or place in the business.

o Have a minimum of 2 questions that you can ask near the conclusion of the interview. Usually, the interviewer will ask if you have any questions. This is your final opportunity to get clarity on any points that will impact your decision to accept the position if offered.

o When the interview has ended, shake hands, use the names of all interviewers and say "thank you for the opportunity to meet today. I really appreciated it. I look forward to hearing from you when you have finalised the interviewing process".

My Top Tips on body language during an interview

You need to walk tall with confidence when you walk into the interview. Have the self-confidence to know that you are the best candidate for the position and your energy will radiate towards those that are interviewing you. Yes, it is natural to be nervous, particularly if you haven't had the opportunity to be part of an interview before.

Although it can feel uncomfortable and unnatural, ask a friend or family member to conduct a mock interview a few hours prior. Any rehearsal will assist you, and this can help calm the nerves.

Interviewers will make a first impression simply from your body language. This will occur the moment you walk in the door to the moment you exit. Body language involves many areas including how you walk, shake hands, eye contact, hand gestures, fidgeting and your overall posture. For example, if you walked into an interview, chin raised high, little eye contact and laying back in the chair with your hands clasped behind your head, your body language would suggest arrogance and not much care. On the other hand, if you walked into the room, smiling, firm handshake, good eye contact and sitting at the front of the chair with your hands placed slightly clasped at the front of the table, the body language would be interpreted completely different. Even if you are not talking, your interviewer will be reading your 'body language'.

Presentation, Preparation and Communication

- The way you present at interview will be a reflection of how you will approach your job in the eyes of those interviewing you. Dress appropriately for the occasion and ensure you remove any piercings that may be offensive to others such as tongue studs or rings through the septum of your nose.

- Completing some prior research/homework on the business or organisation you intend to be employed at before the interview is essential. Being prepared demonstrates pro-activeness and professionalism and interest not just in the position, but in the organisation.

- I recommend printing and taking a copy of your resume and any other written references or information that you may need to refer to during the interview. You may even like to bring along some information about the organisation like a brochure for example.

- When being interviewed, do not use any profanity even if the interviewer uses one.

- Do not use slang. For example, do not use 'yep'

rather than 'yes'.

- Use shared eye contact across all interviewers and not just directed at one person.
- Also, ensure you use great eye contact and avoid looking down when you talk.
- Listen very carefully to the questions being asked and address that question.
- Aim to ask some friendly questions before the interview. This will allow everyone to feel more comfortable before commencing.

Post Interview

Many people underestimate the power of communication and professionalism following their interview. Yes, it is not only what you say and the impression you make on interview day, but what you do with the hours and days that follow.

In several interviews that I have personally been involved with as an employer, there have been situations where there have been two candidates that have performed equally as impressive at the interview. The decision on who to appoint has been divided amongst the interview panel, and the decision has been very difficult. In the end, there is always a deciding factor, and it usually comes down to the final referee checks or equally as important, the communication by the candidate either on the day or within 24 hours of the interview.

These are the qualities that successful candidates have displayed post-interview, and these include:

1. They have written a short and professional email to thank the interviewer or panel for the

opportunity to be part of the interview process. This demonstrated their gratitude and communication skills. The email would usually go something like this:

Dear Brian,

Thank you very much for the opportunity to meet today. I appreciated the opportunity to be part of the interview process and discuss the position of junior administration coordinator.

Please let me know if I can provide anything further to assist with your decision, and I look forward to hearing from you.

Kind Regards,
David Thomson

2. If you are requested to provide additional information including alternative referee names for contact, then action this request promptly.

Other Post Interview Tips

- Don't be too impatient when waiting to hear back on the outcome of the interview. Decisions can take anywhere from 24 hours to 4 weeks, depending on the number of candidates and positions the business is employing. It would be appropriate to make contact two weeks following the interview if you have not had a response with a courteous email or phone call. Respect the answer you are given and then do not make any further contact unless they request additional information from you.

- If you are unsuccessful for the job you have applied for, continue to remain professional. Understandably, you will be disappointed but refrain from saying or doing anything that may jeopardize future applications. Employers will take particular note of those that missed out on a position, and their gracious response to the bad news as this demonstrates strength of character and resilience. You may be surprised how quickly you get a call back with a new opening or opportunity.

Final Reminders

There are many elements involved in being successful for jobs that could potentially lead you to the career of your dreams. This book has provided you with some practical information while other tips are from experts in their fields such as Human Resources Managers plus my personal experiences.

There are 7 Key Tips that I will provide you as final reminders in Job Launch. If you stick to just these 7 tips alone, you will be ready to land your first job or even your dream job!

SOCIAL MEDIA

It is usually a prerequisite for employers to do a check across various social media platforms. If you have photos online, please ensure these photos do not paint you in a negative light. Employers will form an immediate opinion of you either rightly or wrongly purely on your photos or content. I've known of applicants that have immediately been dismissed based on inappropriate photos at parties or other material that should never have made its way online. I'm sure all of you would have been involved in discussions at school regarding the dangers of social media so take it very seriously. You may not fully comprehend it now, but the long-term consequences that can occur from one inappropriate post or photo can cause years of issues along with the fact that you will come across as very unprofessional.

COVER LETTER

If the advertised position requests a cover letter, then tailor the letter specifically for that role. Do not get lazy and fall for the trap of 'reusing' old cover letters for applications. Do not be upset if you are not considered for a position if you have not even followed the guidelines or made an effort to do so. A paragraph note via an online application service is not acceptable. Do it properly and do not be lazy. It may cost you hundreds of thousands of dollars in the long run.

RESUME

Your resume is a direct reflection of you. Use a professional template, ensure the information is easy to read and is current. Have 2 or 3 other people look over your resume to check for grammatical or formatting issues. You can also use a software tool like 'Grammarly' that will check for spelling and grammatical issues.

TIME MANAGEMENT

Be prompt when responding to any form of correspondence be that phone or email messages from a potential employer. If you take too long, you risk your application being discarded.

Please avoid at all costs being late for the interview. You would sooner arrive near the venue 30 minutes prior and be ready rather than panicking and risk being late. If for whatever reason you are running late, always call ahead via phone and notify your interviewer or a member on reception that can pass on the message immediately.

REFEREES

Consider carefully those people you list as referees. They will be critical to your chances of securing an interview if there are several high calibre candidates. Contact your referees as a courtesy to let them know that they may receive a call regarding a position you have applied or interviewed for.

PROFESSIONAL & PRESENTABLE

Remain professional and presentable at all times. This is something you should adopt in general. The way you conduct yourself will build the first impression the moment your application arrives, the moment you walk in for your interview and the day you arrive for the first day of your new job.

BODY LANGUAGE

Your self-confidence will provide magnetic energy to the room if you are confident and smile. Make great eye contact and share it between interviewers, never slouch in your chair and always shake hands firmly.

CONGRATULATIONS

As noted at the very beginning of this book, I have had many employment experiences that have enabled me to gain knowledge, travel, build confidence, develop great contacts, friendships, financial independence and various other life skills and applications. These experiences have led me on the path I am today, and you too will make career choices that will allow you to develop your career journey to share over the years.

The purpose of this book was to provide you with all the tools to give you an excellent head start. The tips and recommendations contained in Job Launch will provide you with an excellent practical guide. Along with these, I also want to provide you with professional templates so you can develop and tailor your cover letters and resume. These will be available via the links on the following pages. I encourage you to make use of them because I know they work have worked for me and many of my students and I know they will work for you too!

I want to wish you the very best with your search, and I hope the information contained has greatly assisted you to *Launch into your career*. All the very best on your journey!

TEMPLATES

Cover Letter Template - appendix 1

<Business Name>   <Your Name>
<Contact Name>   <Address>
<Street Address>   <Contact Phone>
                                          <Contact Email>

<Enter Date>

Position Application

<Enter the Position Name – Business Name>

To whom it may concern <or enter name>,

<complete the body of the text>

.

Thank you for your consideration of my application.

Yours sincerely,

[include signature here]

[Your Name]

Cover Letter Example - appendix 2

The City of Brunswick
Arts and Culture Division
Job Application:
Office Assistant
Cultural Museum

Sonia Kew
11 Beach Road
Mt. Hamilton 4121
P. 0515 623 111
s-kew2001@gmail.com

18th August 2021.

Position Application:
Casual Office Assistant, Cultural Museum

To whom it may concern,

I am writing regarding the casual position of **Office Assistant** at the Cultural Museum as advertised on your website.

I have a strong background working in administrative positions, and this role encompasses several different responsibilities that I have previous experience in.

In my previous role as Reception Coordinator, I was responsible for bookings, checking in and out of guests using the hotel booking software and assisting guests with reservations and airport transfers. This role required flexibility, organization, efficiency and working under pressure situations.

I am currently studying a Bachelor of Education; I have a current First Aid Certificate, and I have participated in various work experience positions in hospitality throughout my schooling.

I enjoy working in a face-paced environment, and I am particularly interested in working in an inclusive and diverse environment. I am very passionate about Arts & Culture, and I believe this role would suit my skill set.

Thank you for your consideration of my application. I look forward to the opportunity to meet regarding the position of Casual Office Assistant at the Cultural Museum.

Yours sincerely,

<insert signature>

Sonia Kew

Job Launch

Resume Template - appendix 3

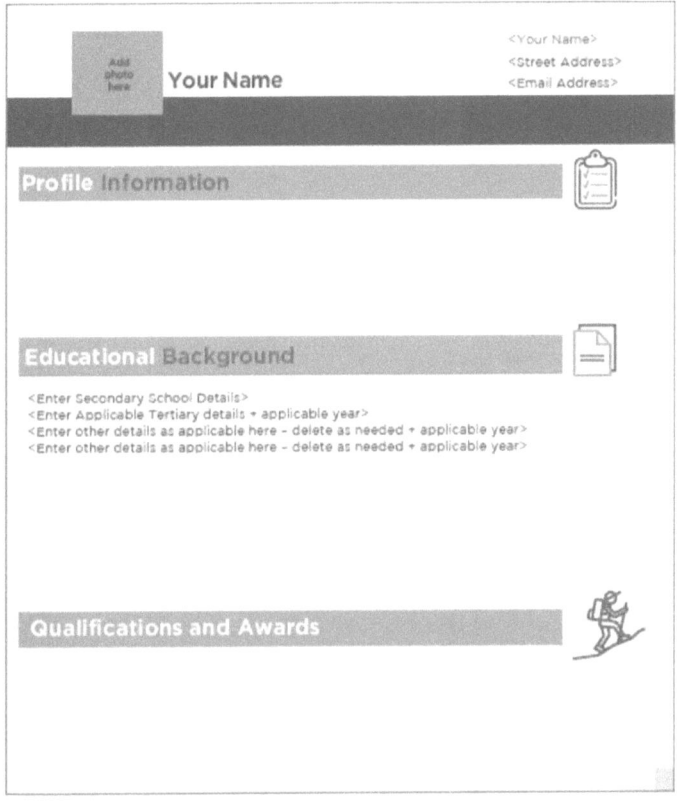

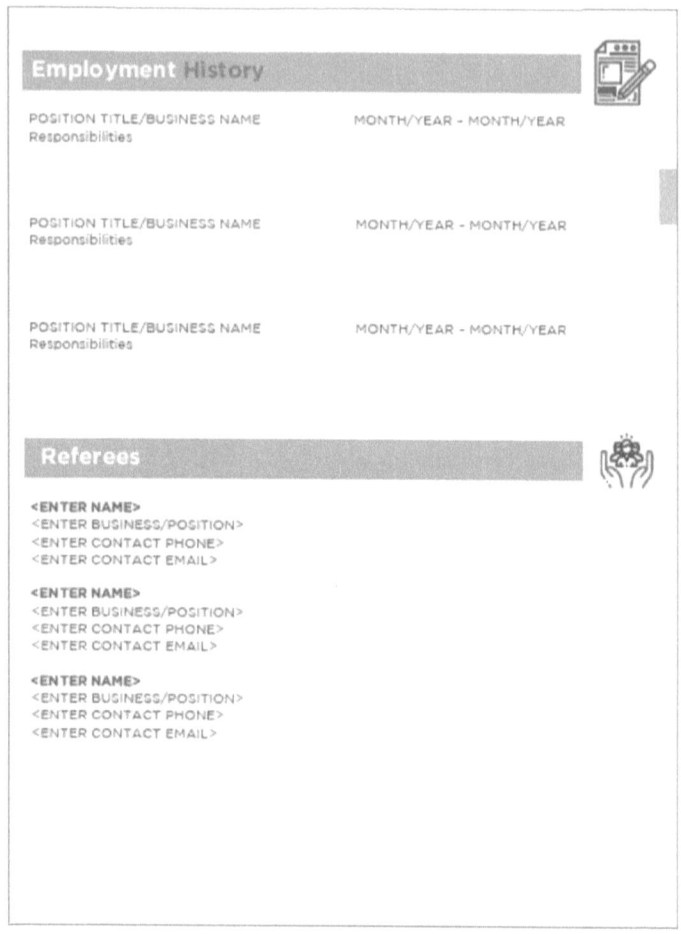

To download and view 3 different resume options for your personal use, please visit the below link:

https://mailchi.mp/2b7889402862/thelifegradua te-resume-template

Books and Resources by Romney Nelson

Magnetic Goals

The Daily Goal Tracker

The Habit Switch

Job Launch

The 5 Year Success Blueprint

<u>Soon to be Released</u>

The Power of the Attraction Mindset

Magnetic Goals

"I found the book engaging, a fast and satisfying read. We hear a lot about setting goals. The author gets to the tactical details (Reverse Planning), habits, attitude, and mindset to cultivate to make your success predictable. I've heard bits and pieces of those things from other books and mentors but have never read them collected in a readable, actionable, step by step manual.

I picked up the book a few days ago while in an early morning funk. After about a half-hour of reading, I felt ready to take on the day. What's more, I knew what steps to take that I had been missing. If you feel stopped and want to move in new directions, read this book and apply the steps. It's made a difference for me in just a few days!"

5 Stars - Jim Christenson

The Daily Goal Tracker

"This amazing book, 'The Daily Goal Tracker', is an extraordinary resource that shows you how to set your goals, organize your life, double and triple your income, and achieve more, faster, than you ever thought possible."

Brian Tracy – International Motivational Speaker and author of 80+ books

"I highly recommend this book. I found it to be a good read as well as extremely helpful with structuring and preparing my goals."

5 Stars - Deanne Barberlogou
Sales Account Manager

The Habit Switch

AMAZON #1 Best-Seller

Habit is definitely a buzzword these days. But I think the author has a unique spin on this well-worn topic. He suggests making small, incremental changes that focus on the long-term benefits for health. There's no big makeover you have to attempt all at once. I like that he advises steering clear of the latest trends and gurus in the health field, and his approach is that both diet and exercise be sustainable for long-term health. As such, he doesn't espouse fad diets or no-pain-no-gain exercising. Interestingly, in the beginning, he details his own daily routine and healthful habits that he has incorporated into his life. He has a couple of systems that are unique to him, including an actually trademarked one called DR. ACTION, which is like SMART goals on steroids but to be used at a personal level, not at an Institutional one (which is always how SMART goals struck me). He also has a system of how you choose your goals that he calls Stop, Review, Pivot, and Power, which helps you figure out where you're at and where you might want to be. All in all, I found this to be a fascinating read that engages you to think about the various aspects of your health and what they could mean to you, and then it gives you some tools to help implement the incremental habits that you deem relevant and worthwhile to your health.

5 Stars – Jamie B – Amazon Top 500 Reviewer

The 5 Year Blueprint

Job Launch

The Power of the Attraction Mindset

Please Leave a Review

I would greatly appreciate if you enjoyed this book to leave a review on Amazon. Reviews will assist **Magnetic Goals** to reach more people for a positive impact on their lives.

You may also be interested in joining the EXCLUSIVE Review Team to receive future books in return for leaving an honest review.

To leave a review, please visit www.amazon.com and to apply to be part of the Book Review Team please email info@thelifegraduate.com with the subject heading: **Review Team EOI**.

About the Author

Romney is the founder of The Life Graduate and author of Magnetic Goals and The Daily Goal Tracker. He is regarded as one of the leading experts in goal setting and daily habits with the development of the unique **Dr ACTION**™ and **'THE GOAL LOOP'** systems. He has represented Australia in sport, is an executive business coach, speaker, qualified teacher and Personal Trainer and owner of two rapidly growing businesses in the educational space.

Romney has previously held Head of Faculty positions in some of the most prestigious schools in Australia and has also held senior executive positions in several businesses including a current advisory role for Australia's largest provider of mobile dental to schools.

Romney has dedicated the past 20 years to helping others achieve success and fulfilment in their lives through his coaching, teaching, masterclasses, mentoring, resources and books. His clients speak of his passion and dedication for self-improvement and bringing that knowledge and experience to help others achieve what they want in their lives.

Please refer to the below details to reach out to Romney for speaking engagements, podcasts or other media requests.

Web. www.thelifegraduate.com
Email. info@thelifegraduate.com
LinkedIn. Romney Nelson

Resources

https://content.wisestep.com/body-language-dos-and-donts-in-job-interviews/

https://www.indeed.com/career-advice/resumes-cover-letters/10-resume-writing-tips

https://victorsykes.com/wpcontent/uploads/2019/01/The-Simple-and-Powerful-Word-to-Use-to-Become-High-Status.pdf